THE SPICE CABINET APOTHECARY

THE SPICE CABINET APOTHECARY: NATURAL HEALTH AT YOUR FINGERTIPS

BY: RICHARD D. KRAUSE

<u>Preface</u>

Imagine a summer's morning in the picturesque Alleghany Mountains of Western Pennsylvania, where the day is kissed by the gentle warmth of the sun. Nature is alive, and the world awakens to a symphony of tranquility. A silver lake reflects the azure sky, and a delicate mist dances above it. Dew-kissed meadow grass and the lush foliage glisten in the soft morning light.

In this serene setting, a scene unfolds. A kindly, white-haired man, deeply connected to the land, makes his way through the abundant undergrowth. His attire is practical—a white linen shirt open at the neck, khaki pants, and boots dampened by the dew. His presence exudes harmony with the natural world that envelops him.

A young boy, brimming with curiosity, follows closely in his footsteps. They pause by a cluster of blossoming shrubs, and the man bends down, as if introducing an old friend to the boy.

"Look here," he says, his voice filled with warmth and wisdom, "this fragrant plant is

American Angelica. A tea made from it will quickly restore your appetite if you've lost it."

The boy, captivated by the man's knowledge and the plant's potential as a remedy, listens intently. He soaks up every word, realizing that this wisdom is a gift—a legacy from one generation to the next.

That man was Arno Krause—a man of many facets: an artist, an adventurer, an outdoorsman, and a world traveler. To me, he was simply Grandfather. Born and raised in the enchanting Black Forest region of Germany, he embarked on grand adventures in his youth, journeying through the Orient, Africa, and South America. Eventually, he found his way to America, settling in the verdant embrace of the Western Pennsylvania mountains.

That morning stroll in the woods with my Grandfather unfolded nearly seventy plus years ago. It marked the beginning of a lifelong fascination with herbs. Subsequent morning excursions deepened that connection and expanded my knowledge.

Now, more than seven decades later, at the gentle urging of my youngest daughter, I found myself reflecting on those cherished memories. "Dad," she said a few years ago, "you need to write down all this wisdom you carry with you, so we can cherish it when you're no longer here." Our conversation arose after I brewed her a cup of peppermint and parsley tea to soothe her upset stomach. It was that moment—the recognition that this knowledge should not be lost—that inspired me to share it with others.

As you embark on the pages of this eBook, you'll journey through the world of herbs and spices, discovering their remarkable potential for enhancing your well-being. The wisdom passed down from my Grandfather, Arno Krause, lives on through these words. I hope you find this knowledge not only helpful but also deeply fascinating. May it enrich your life, just as it has enriched mine, and connect you with the beauty and healing power of the natural world.

Warm regards,

Richard Douglas Krause]

Chapter 1: Introduction to the Spice Cabinet Apothecary

Welcome to a journey of natural health and well-being, where the simple spices and herbs you have in your kitchen cabinet become powerful allies in your quest for a healthier life. In this chapter, we'll lay the foundation for your spice cabinet apothecary adventure. You'll discover the incredible potential of these everyday ingredients and gain a deeper understanding of the world of herbal medicine. So, let's get started on this flavorful and fragrant path to wellness!

The Power of Kitchen Herbs

When you think of your kitchen spice cabinet, what comes to mind? Perhaps it's a collection of small jars filled with a colorful array of herbs and spices, waiting to enhance your culinary creations. But what if I told you that these same spices and herbs could also enhance your well-being? That's right! The very same ingredients you use to season your meals can also serve as your personal apothecary, providing natural remedies for a variety of health concerns.

For centuries, humans have turned to the healing properties of plants to alleviate ailments and promote health. This ancient wisdom has been passed down through generations and is now at your fingertips in the form of the herbs and spices found in your kitchen.

Understanding Herbal Medicine

Before we dive into the world of spice cabinet apothecaries, it's essential to understand the principles of herbal medicine. Herbalism is the practice of using plants, specifically their leaves, stems, roots, seeds, and even flowers, for medicinal purposes. It's a holistic approach to health that embraces the idea of the interconnectedness of mind, body, and nature.

Here are a few fundamental concepts to keep in mind:

Holistic Wellness

Herbal medicine looks at the whole person, not just the symptoms of an illness. It considers your physical, emotional, and mental well-being as interconnected aspects of your overall health. The goal is not merely to treat a specific ailment but to support your body in achieving and maintaining balance.

The Wisdom of Tradition

Herbal remedies have been used for thousands of years in various cultures around the world. These traditional practices have withstood the test of time, and many herbs have a long history of safe and effective use.

The Synergy of Nature

Herbs contain a complex mix of chemical compounds that work together synergistically to produce their therapeutic effects. This means that the whole plant often has a more significant impact than isolated compounds. It's a beautiful example of nature's wisdom.

Complementary to Modern Medicine

Herbal medicine can complement conventional medical treatments. Many people use herbs in conjunction with pharmaceuticals to enhance their overall health and well-being. However, it's essential to consult with a healthcare professional before making any significant changes to your healthcare regimen.

Your Spice Cabinet: A Treasure Trove of Health

Now, let's turn our attention to your spice cabinet. Open it up, and you'll find a wealth of aromatic treasures waiting to be explored. The spices and herbs you've collected over time aren't just there to add flavor to your dishes; they can also add vitality to your life.

Variety and Versatility

The beauty of a spice cabinet apothecary is its diversity. From the fiery warmth of cinnamon to the soothing embrace of chamomile, your collection offers an array of flavors, scents, and therapeutic potential. This versatility allows you to tailor your herbal remedies to your specific needs.

Everyday Accessibility

Unlike some specialized herbal remedies that require hard-to-find ingredients, the herbs and spices in your kitchen cabinet are readily available and affordable. You don't need to scour the Earth for exotic plants; your spice rack holds the key to natural health.

Empowerment through Knowledge

One of the most empowering aspects of creating a spice cabinet apothecary is the knowledge you gain. As you learn about the properties and uses of different herbs, you become the steward of your well-being. You can make informed choices about your health and the health of your loved ones.

What to Expect in This Book

In the pages that follow, we'll delve into the world of kitchen herbs and spices as natural remedies. Each chapter will focus on a specific aspect of health and well-being, introducing you to the herbs and spices that can make a difference. You'll find practical recipes, tips, and guidance on incorporating these herbs into your daily life.

Whether you're looking to boost your immune system, ease digestive discomfort, reduce stress, or address a particular health concern, we've got you covered. By the time you finish this book, you'll have a well-rounded understanding of herbal medicine and a toolkit of herbal remedies you can use with confidence.

So, are you ready to embark on this flavorful journey to natural health? The Spice Cabinet Apothecary is here to empower you, inspire you, and guide you toward a healthier, more vibrant life. Let's get started!

Chapter 2: Building Your Herbal Toolkit

Welcome back to your spice cabinet apothecary adventure! Now that you've been introduced to the incredible potential of kitchen herbs and spices, it's time to build your herbal toolkit. In this chapter, we'll explore the essential herbs and spices you'll want to have on hand, the tools and equipment you'll need, and how to source and store these botanical treasures. Let's get started on creating your own personal apothecary!

Essential Spices and Herbs

Your spice cabinet likely holds a variety of herbs and spices, each with its unique flavor profile and potential health benefits. While there's a vast world of herbs out there, let's start by focusing on some of the essentials that you'll find in many kitchens:

Cinnamon: This sweet and aromatic spice is known for its anti-inflammatory and antioxidant properties. It's excellent for adding flavor to both sweet and savory dishes.

Turmeric: With its vibrant yellow color, turmeric is a powerhouse of anti-inflammatory and antioxidant compounds. It's often used in curries and gives a warm, earthy flavor.

Ginger: A zesty and warming spice, ginger is celebrated for its digestive benefits and anti-nausea properties. It can be used in teas, stir-fries, and baked goods.

Garlic: Beyond its savory flavor, garlic is renowned for its immune-boosting and heart-healthy properties. Fresh garlic or garlic powder can be used in countless recipes.

Oregano: This fragrant herb is rich in antioxidants and antimicrobial compounds. It's a staple in Italian cuisine and perfect for seasoning sauces and roasted vegetables.

Rosemary: Known for its distinct pine-like aroma, rosemary has anti-inflammatory properties and is often used to flavor roasted meats, potatoes, and bread.

Thyme: With its earthy and slightly minty flavor, thyme is a source of vitamins and minerals. It pairs well with a variety of dishes, from soups to roasted chicken.

Peppermint: This refreshing herb can soothe digestive discomfort and alleviate headaches.

Enjoy it as a tea or use it to flavor desserts and beverages.

Cayenne Pepper: Known for its fiery heat, cayenne contains capsaicin, which may support metabolism and pain relief. Use it sparingly to add a kick to your dishes.

Basil: This aromatic herb adds a burst of fresh flavor to salads, pasta, and sauces. It's also believed to have anti-inflammatory properties.

Remember that these are just a few examples, and your spice cabinet may contain many more herbs and spices with unique health benefits. As you explore herbal medicine, you'll discover the specific properties of each plant and how they can address various health concerns.

Tools and Equipment

Creating your spice cabinet apothecary doesn't require an extensive collection of specialized tools. In fact, you likely already have most of what you need in your kitchen. Here are some essential tools and equipment to have on hand:

Mortar and Pestle: This age-old tool is perfect for grinding herbs and spices into a fine powder or paste. It allows you to release the aromatic oils and medicinal compounds locked within the plants.

Airtight Containers: To preserve the freshness and potency of your herbs and spices, invest in airtight glass or plastic containers. Label them with the name and date of purchase.

Measuring Spoons and Cups: Accurate measurements are crucial when creating herbal remedies. Keep a set of measuring spoons and cups specifically for your herbal preparations.

Strainers and Cheesecloth: When making herbal infusions or tinctures, you'll need a strainer or cheesecloth to separate the liquid from the plant material.

Glass Jars for Infusions: For longer-term herbal infusions, glass jars with tight-sealing lids are ideal. They allow you to steep herbs in a carrier liquid like alcohol or oil.

A Grater or Zester: If you're working with fresh herbs and spices like ginger or citrus zest, a grater or zester will come in handy.

Knife and Cutting Board: For chopping and preparing fresh herbs, a sharp knife and a clean cutting board are essential.

Small Funnel: When transferring herbal preparations to bottles or containers, a small funnel makes the process much neater.

Sourcing and Storing Herbs

Now that you know what tools and herbs you need, it's time to think about sourcing and storing these precious botanicals.

Sourcing Herbs:

When it comes to sourcing herbs and spices for your spice cabinet apothecary, you have a few options:

Local Grocery Stores: Most basic herbs and spices are readily available at your local grocery store. Look for organic options when possible.

Farmers' Markets: Farmers' markets often offer fresh, locally grown herbs that can be a delightful addition to your apothecary.

Online Retailers: Many online retailers specialize in herbs and spices, offering a wide selection of both common and rare varieties. Be sure to read reviews and check the source's reputation.

Grow Your Own: If you have a green thumb, consider growing your herbs in a garden or even in pots on your windowsill.

Fresh herbs are a wonderful addition to your herbal toolkit.

Storing Herbs:

Proper storage is crucial to maintain the flavor and potency of your herbs and spices. Here's how to do it:

Keep it Cool and Dark: Store your herbs in a cool, dark place away from direct sunlight and heat sources. Light and heat can cause herbs to lose their flavor and effectiveness.

Use Airtight Containers: As mentioned earlier, airtight glass or plastic containers are perfect for storing dried herbs and spices. This prevents moisture and air from degrading them.

Label Everything: Make sure to label your containers with the name of the herb or spice and the date of purchase. This helps you keep track of freshness.

Store Fresh Herbs Properly: If you're working with fresh herbs, wrap them in a damp paper towel, place them in a plastic bag, and refrigerate. Use them as quickly as possible for the best flavor.

Rotate Your Stock: Spices and herbs don't last forever. Over time, they can lose their potency. Make sure to periodically assess and replace older herbs and spices.

The Journey Begins

Congratulations! You now have the foundational knowledge and tools to start building your spice cabinet apothecary. In the chapters that follow, we'll explore how to put these herbs and spices to use in a variety of natural remedies and recipes for better health.

In the next chapter, we'll dive into the basics of herbal preparations and methods, teaching you how to harness the healing power of your botanical treasures. So, get ready to infuse your life with the magic of herbs and spices as we continue on this flavorful journey to natural health!

Chapter 3: Herbal Basics

Welcome back to your spice cabinet apothecary adventure! In this chapter, we're going to delve into the fundamental principles of herbal medicine. Understanding the basics is crucial as it forms the foundation for harnessing the healing power of your kitchen herbs and spices. So, let's get started on this journey of discovery!

Herbal Preparations and Methods

Before you can create effective herbal remedies, it's essential to understand the various ways you can prepare and use herbs. Here are some common herbal preparations and methods you'll encounter:

1. Infusions:

- **What it is:** An infusion is a method of extracting the beneficial compounds from dried herbs by steeping them in hot water.

- **How to make it:** Boil water, pour it over the herbs, and cover the container to steep. After a specified time, strain and enjoy the liquid.
- **Best for:** Infusions are perfect for delicate herbs like chamomile and mint, as well as for making herbal teas.

2. Decoctions:

- **What it is:** Decoctions are similar to infusions, but they involve simmering tougher plant parts like roots, bark, or seeds in water for an extended period.
- **How to make it:** Place the herbs in cold water, bring it to a boil, and then simmer for a set time before straining.
- **Best for:** Decoctions are suitable for extracting compounds from tougher plant materials.

3. Tinctures:

- **What it is:** A tincture is a concentrated liquid herbal extract made by soaking herbs in alcohol (I have found that Vodka or EverPure works the best) or a glycerin-water mixture (You could also use a good grade of Virgin Olive Oil).
- Do not use rubbing or denatured alcohol! They are poisonous!
- **How to make it:** Fill a glass jar with herbs and cover them with alcohol or glycerin-water. Let it sit for several weeks, shaking it occasionally, before straining.

- **Best for:** Tinctures are ideal for preserving herbs long-term and providing a potent, easily dosable form of herbal medicine.

4. Salves and Balms:

- *What it is:* Salves and balms are topical preparations made by infusing herbs into oils or fats and then solidifying them.
- *How to make it:* Heat herbs and oils together to infuse, then strain and mix with beeswax or other solidifying agents also due to it's unique healing properties I have found that mixing abit of Honey into these is very helpful, it is a natural disinvectant.
- *Best for:* Salves and balms are excellent for skin conditions, muscle and joint pain, and wound healing.

5. Poultices and Compresses:

- *What it is:* Poultices involve applying mashed or heated herbs directly to the skin, while compresses use cloth soaked in a strong herbal infusion.
- *How to make it:* For a poultice, mash fresh or dried herbs and apply directly to the affected area. For a compress, soak a cloth in an herbal infusion and apply it to the skin.
- *Best for:* Poultices and compresses are used for localized issues like bruises, sprains, and skin irritations.

6. Capsules and Tablets:

- *What it is:* You can encapsulate powdered herbs or create tablets for convenient oral consumption.
- *How to make it:* Purchase empty capsules or use a tablet press to create your herbal supplements.
- *Best for:* Capsules and tablets are perfect for herbs with strong flavors or for precise dosing.

7. Syrups and Elixirs:

- *What it is:* Syrups and elixirs are sweet herbal preparations that combine herbs with honey, sugar, or other sweeteners.
- *How to make it:* Infuse herbs in a sweet liquid, strain, and add a sweetener. Syrups are often thicker than elixirs.
- *Best for:* Syrups and elixirs are a pleasant way to administer herbs, particularly for children.

8. Powders:

- *What it is:* Herbs can be dried and ground into a fine powder for various applications.
- *How to make it:* Dry herbs thoroughly and grind them into a powder using a mortar and pestle or a spice grinder.
- *Best for:* Powders are versatile and can be used in culinary dishes, capsules, or as topical applications.

These methods offer a range of options for preparing and using herbs, allowing you to choose the most suitable approach for your needs and the specific herbs you're working with.

Dosage and Safety Considerations

While herbs can be incredibly beneficial, it's important to approach them with care, especially if you're new to herbal medicine. Here are some essential dosage and safety considerations: If you are taking prescription medications always check with your health care provider before starting any herbal regiment.

1. **Start Low and Go Slow**: When trying a new herb, start with a small dose and gradually increase it if needed. This approach allows you to gauge your body's response and avoid potential adverse effects.

2. **Consult with a Professional**: If you have underlying health conditions, are pregnant or nursing, or are taking medications, consult with a qualified healthcare practitioner before using herbs as a remedy. They can help you navigate potential interactions and contraindications.

3. **Quality Matters**: Choose high-quality, organic herbs whenever possible. Quality can

significantly impact the effectiveness of herbal remedies.

4. Know Your Allergies: Be aware of any allergies you may have to herbs or related plants. Cross-reactivity can occur with certain botanicals.

5. Respect Medicinal Herbs: Treat herbs with the same respect you would pharmaceuticals. They have the potential to cause harm if not used appropriately.

6. Research and Education: Continuously educate yourself about the herbs you're using. Understanding their properties, potential side effects, and contraindications is crucial.

7. Keep Records: Maintain a record of the herbs you use, their dosages, and your experiences with them. This information can be valuable for tracking your health progress.

Herbal Terminology

As you dive deeper into the world of herbal medicine, you'll encounter specific terminology that's used to describe herbs and their properties. Here are some key terms to familiarize yourself with:

1. Constituents: These are the chemical compounds found within herbs that give them their therapeutic properties. Examples include alkaloids, flavonoids, and essential oils.

2. Actions: Actions refer to what a herb does in the body. For example, an herb can have anti-inflammatory, diuretic, or nervine actions.

3. Indications: Indications are the specific conditions or symptoms that an herb is known to address. For example, an herb might be indicated for insomnia, digestive discomfort, or respiratory congestion.

4. Contraindications: Contraindications are situations or conditions in which the use of a particular herb is not recommended. For instance, some herbs are contraindicated during pregnancy or with certain medications.

5. Adaptogen: Adaptogens are a class of herbs that help the body adapt to stress and maintain balance. They're known for their ability to support the body's natural resilience.

6. Infusion vs. Decoction: As mentioned earlier, an infusion involves steeping herbs in hot water, while a decoction involves simmering them. Understanding the difference is essential for proper preparation.

7. Spectrum of Use: Herbs can have a broad or narrow spectrum of use. Some herbs are versatile and can address a wide range of conditions, while others have a more specific focus.

8. Synergy: Synergy refers to the idea that the combined action of multiple herbs can be more potent or effective than the sum of their individual actions.

Your Journey of Herbal Discovery

With a solid understanding of herbal preparations, dosage considerations, and key terminology, you're well-equipped to embark on your journey of herbal discovery. In the chapters that follow, we'll explore specific herbs and spices, their properties, and practical recipes for using them to address common health concerns.

As you delve into the world of herbal medicine, remember that it's a journey of learning and exploration. Each herb has its own story to tell and unique contributions to make to your well-being. So, embrace this opportunity to connect with the wisdom of nature and harness the healing power of your spice cabinet apothecary.

In the next chapter, we'll explore the art of using kitchen herbs and spices to boost your

immune system and stay healthy throughout
the year. Get ready to unlock the natural
immunity-boosting potential of your spice
cabinet!

Chapter 4: Immune-Boosting Herbs

Welcome back to your spice cabinet apothecary journey! In this chapter, we're going to explore the wonderful world of immune-boosting herbs. Your immune system is your body's natural defense against illnesses and infections, and these herbs can be your allies in keeping it strong and resilient. So, let's dive into the flavorful and aromatic world of herbs that support your immune health.

Understanding the Immune System

Before we get into the specific herbs, let's take a moment to understand how your immune system works. Your immune system is a complex network of cells, tissues, and organs that work together to defend your body against harmful invaders like bacteria, viruses, and other pathogens

Here's a simplified overview of how it functions:

1. **Recognition:** Your immune system can recognize foreign substances in your body,

distinguishing them from your own healthy cells.

2. **Attack:** Once identified, your immune system mounts an attack against the invaders. This can involve various immune cells and molecules working together to neutralize or destroy the threat.

3. **Memory:** Your immune system has a memory. If it encounters the same pathogen again, it can respond more quickly and effectively, often preventing illness or reducing its severity.

4. **Balance:** A healthy immune system strikes a delicate balance between attacking harmful invaders and leaving your body's own cells untouched. This balance is essential to prevent autoimmune diseases, where the immune system mistakenly attacks healthy tissue.

Immune-Boosting Herbs in Your Spice Cabinet

Now that you have a basic understanding of how your immune system functions, let's explore some immune-boosting herbs that you may already have in your spice cabinet:

1. Garlic (Allium sativum):

- **Immune Benefits:** Garlic has antibacterial and antiviral properties that can help your body fend off infections. It also supports the production of immune-boosting white blood cells.

- **How to Use:** Incorporate garlic into your daily cooking, or make a potent garlic honey by steeping crushed garlic in honey.

2. Ginger (Zingiber officinale):

- **Immune Benefits:** Ginger has antioxidant and anti-inflammatory properties that support immune function. It can also help soothe symptoms of respiratory infections.
- **How to Use:** Add fresh ginger to teas, soups, or stir-fries. You can also make ginger shots or syrups.

3. Turmeric (Curcuma longa):

- **Immune Benefits:** Curcumin, the active compound in turmeric, has powerful anti-inflammatory and antioxidant properties. It can help regulate the immune response.
- **How to Use:** Make golden milk by mixing turmeric, milk (or a dairy-free alternative), and honey. You can also add turmeric to curries and soups.

4. Cinnamon (Cinnamomum verum or Cinnamomum cassia):

- **Immune Benefits:** Cinnamon is rich in antioxidants and has anti-inflammatory properties. It may help boost the immune system and combat infections.

- **How to Use:** Sprinkle cinnamon on oatmeal, yogurt, or your morning coffee. You can also make a cinnamon tea or infusion.

5. Oregano (Origanum vulgare):

- **Immune Benefits:** Oregano is a potent herb with antimicrobial properties. It can help fight off bacterial and viral infections.
- **How to Use:** Use dried oregano in Italian dishes, soups, or as a seasoning for roasted vegetables. Oregano oil is also available as a supplement.

6. Thyme (Thymus vulgaris):

- **Immune Benefits:** Thyme contains thymol, a compound with antimicrobial properties. It can help combat infections and soothe coughs and sore throats.
- **How to Use:** Add fresh or dried thyme to stews, roasts, or herbal teas.

7. Cayenne Pepper (Capsicum annuum):

- **Immune Benefits:** Cayenne contains capsaicin, which has anti-inflammatory and immune-boosting properties. It may also help clear congestion.
- **How to Use:** Add a pinch of cayenne to soups, sauces, or even a cup of warm water with lemon and honey.

8. Rosemary (Rosmarinus officinalis):

- **Immune Benefits:** Rosemary has antioxidant and anti-inflammatory properties that can support overall health, including the immune system.
- **How to Use:** Use fresh or dried rosemary in roasted meats, potatoes, or as a seasoning for bread.

9. Sage (Salvia officinalis):

- **Immune Benefits:** Sage has antimicrobial properties and can help soothe sore throats and coughs. It's also rich in antioxidants.
- **How to Use:** Make sage tea by steeping fresh or dried sage leaves. You can also incorporate sage into savory dishes.

Recipes for Immune Health

Now that you know which herbs can boost your immune system, let's explore some practical recipes to incorporate them into your daily routine:

1. Garlic and Honey Immune Tonic:

- **Ingredients:** 1 bulb of garlic, 1 cup of honey

- Instructions: Peel and crush the garlic cloves. Combine them with honey in a glass jar. Let it sit for a few days before using. Take a teaspoon daily for immune support.

2. Ginger Turmeric Tea:

- Ingredients: 1-inch piece of fresh ginger, 1 teaspoon of ground turmeric, 1 teaspoon of honey, 1 lemon slice
- Instructions: Grate the ginger into a cup, add turmeric, and pour hot water over them. Add honey and a lemon slice. Steep for a few minutes and enjoy.

3. Cinnamon Oatmeal:

- Ingredients: Rolled oats, milk (or dairy-free alternative), honey, and a sprinkle of cinnamon
- Instructions: Cook the oats with milk, drizzle with honey, and sprinkle cinnamon on top for a comforting and immune-boosting breakfast.

4. Oregano-Infused Oil:

- Ingredients: Dried oregano leaves, olive oil
- Instructions: Fill a glass jar with dried oregano and cover it with olive oil. Seal and let it sit in a cool, dark place for a week. Use this oil for salad dressings or drizzling over dishes.

5. Thyme and Honey Cough Syrup:

- Ingredients: Fresh thyme sprigs, honey

- Instructions: Fill a jar with fresh thyme sprigs and cover them with honey. Let it sit for a few days. Take a teaspoon as needed to soothe coughs.

6. Cayenne Lemonade:

- Ingredients: Lemon juice, water, honey, a pinch of cayenne
- Instructions: Mix lemon juice, water, honey, and a pinch of cayenne for a zesty immune-boosting drink.

7. Rosemary Roasted Vegetables:

- Ingredients: Assorted vegetables, olive oil, fresh rosemary leaves
- Instructions: Toss vegetables with olive oil and fresh rosemary leaves. Roast in the oven for a flavorful and nutritious side dish.

8. Sage and Lemon Throat Soothing Tea:

- Ingredients: Fresh or dried sage leaves, lemon juice, honey
- Instructions: Steep sage leaves in hot water, add lemon juice and honey. Sip this soothing tea to ease a sore throat.

9. Peppermint Infused Water:

- **Ingredients:** Fresh peppermint leaves, water, ice
- **Instructions:** Add fresh peppermint leaves to a glass of water with ice for a refreshing and immune-boosting drink. Add a honey to your taste for a healthy sweetness.

Remember that these recipes are just a starting point. Feel free to get creative and experiment with these immune-boosting herbs in your favorite dishes and beverages.

A Flavorful Defense

As you explore the world of immune-boosting herbs, you'll not only enhance your culinary creations but also strengthen your body's natural defense mechanisms. These herbs, with their rich flavors and aromatic profiles, offer a delightful way to support your immune system year-round.

In the next chapter, we'll turn our attention to digestive health and discover how kitchen herbs and spices can soothe digestive discomfort and promote overall well-being. Get ready to enjoy the comforting and flavorful remedies that your spice cabinet apothecary has to offer!

Chapter 5: Digestive Harmony with Kitchen Herbs

Welcome back to your spice cabinet apothecary adventure! In this chapter, we're going to explore the wonderful world of digestive health and discover how kitchen herbs and spices can help you achieve and maintain a harmonious digestive system. So, if you've ever experienced digestive discomfort or simply want to promote overall well-being, read on to unlock the secrets of culinary herbal remedies.

The Importance of Digestive Health

Your digestive system is a marvel of intricate processes and organs working together to break down food, absorb nutrients, and eliminate waste. When it functions smoothly, you often take it for granted. However, when digestive issues arise, they can affect your overall well-being and quality of life.

Digestive health matters because:

- **Nutrient Absorption:** Your digestive system is responsible for extracting vital nutrients from the food you eat and delivering them to your cells. Without proper digestion, nutrient deficiencies can occur.
- **Immune Function:** A significant portion of your immune system resides in your gut. A healthy digestive system supports a robust immune response.
- **Mood and Brain Health:** The gut-brain connection is well-documented. A balanced digestive system can positively impact mood and cognitive function.
- **Energy Levels:** Efficient digestion ensures the energy you need for daily activities.
- Comfort: Digestive comfort is essential for overall well-being and quality of life.

Common Digestive Issues

Digestive discomfort can manifest in various ways, from occasional gas and bloating to more chronic conditions like irritable bowel syndrome (IBS) or acid reflux. Here are some common digestive issues:

1. **Indigestion:** Also known as dyspepsia, indigestion can result from overeating, eating too quickly, or consuming spicy or fatty foods. It often leads to symptoms like bloating, heartburn, and discomfort.

2. **Gas and Bloating:** Gas in the digestive tract can cause bloating and discomfort. It may result from certain foods, swallowing air while eating, or bacterial fermentation in the gut.

3. **Constipation:** Difficulty passing stools or infrequent bowel movements can lead to constipation. It's often linked to a lack of dietary fiber, dehydration, or a sedentary lifestyle.

4. **Diarrhea:** Loose or watery stools can result from various factors, including infections, food intolerances, or stress.

5. **Irritable Bowel Syndrome (IBS):** IBS is a chronic condition characterized by abdominal pain, bloating, and altered bowel habits. It can be triggered or exacerbated by stress, certain foods, or hormonal changes.

6. **Gastroesophageal Reflux Disease (GERD):** GERD is a chronic condition in which stomach acid flows back into the esophagus, causing heartburn and irritation.

Herbal Allies for Digestive Health

The good news is that many kitchen herbs and spices can come to the rescue when it comes to digestive discomfort. Let's explore some of these herbal allies and their digestive benefits:

Peppermint (Mentha × piperita):

- **Digestive Benefits**: Peppermint can relax the muscles of the gastrointestinal tract, reducing spasms and gas. It's particularly helpful for indigestion and irritable bowel syndrome (IBS).
- **How to Use:** Brew peppermint tea or add fresh peppermint leaves to your meals and beverages.

Ginger (Zingiber officinale):

- **Digestive Benefits:** Ginger can stimulate digestion, reduce nausea, and ease inflammation in the digestive tract. It's excellent for motion sickness and indigestion.
- **How to Use:** Sip on ginger tea, add fresh ginger to your cooking, or chew on a small piece of ginger.

Fennel (Foeniculum vulgare):

- **Digestive Benefits:** Fennel can relieve gas, bloating, and indigestion. It's often used to ease colic in infants and soothe digestive discomfort in adults.
- **How to Use:** Chew on fennel seeds after meals or brew fennel tea.

Chamomile (Matricaria chamomilla):

- **Digestive Benefits:** Chamomile has anti-inflammatory and calming properties that can soothe an upset stomach and reduce indigestion.
- **How to Use:** Make chamomile tea by steeping dried chamomile flowers in hot water.

Cumin (Cuminum cyminum):

- **Digestive Benefits:** Cumin seeds can stimulate the production of digestive enzymes and alleviate gas and bloating.
- **How to Use:** Toast cumin seeds and add them to dishes like rice, soups, or stews.

Coriander (Coriandrum sativum):

- **Digestive Benefits:** Coriander can ease digestive discomfort, reduce gas, and promote healthy bowel movements.
- **How to Use:** Crush coriander seeds and use them as a spice in cooking or make coriander tea.

Turmeric (Curcuma longa):

- **Digestive Benefits:** Turmeric's anti-inflammatory properties can help reduce inflammation in the digestive tract and soothe symptoms of indigestion.
- **How to Use:** Incorporate turmeric into your cooking or make a turmeric-infused tea.

Dill (Anethum graveolens):

- **Digestive Benefits:** Dill can ease digestive discomfort, reduce gas, and stimulate digestion.
- **How to Use:** Use fresh dill leaves as a garnish or brew dill tea from seeds or leaves.

Cinnamon (Cinnamomum verum or Cinnamomum cassia):

- **Digestive Benefits:** Cinnamon can alleviate indigestion and bloating by promoting the efficient breakdown of food.
- **How to Use:** Add a pinch of cinnamon to your meals, beverages, or herbal teas.

Licorice (Glycyrrhiza glabra):

- **Digestive Benefits:** Licorice root can soothe the digestive tract and help with symptoms of acid reflux and indigestion.
- **How to Use:** Brew licorice tea or use licorice root as an infusion.

Recipes for Digestive Wellness

Now that you're familiar with these digestive-friendly herbs, let's explore some practical recipes to support digestive harmony:

Peppermint and Ginger Tea:

- **Ingredients:** Fresh peppermint leaves, fresh ginger slices, hot water, honey (optional)
- **Instructions:** Steep peppermint and ginger in hot water. Add honey if desired. Sip this soothing tea after meals.

Fennel Digestive Infusion:

- **Ingredients:** Fennel seeds, hot water
- **Instructions:** Steep fennel seeds in hot water for a mild, digestive infusion. Sip it throughout the day.

Chamomile and Cinnamon Soothing Tea:

- **Ingredients:** Chamomile flowers, a pinch of cinnamon, hot water, honey (optional)
- **Instructions:** Steep chamomile flowers and cinnamon in hot water. Add honey if desired. Enjoy this calming tea before bedtime.

Ginger and Turmeric Tonic:

- **Ingredients:** Fresh ginger, ground turmeric, hot water, honey (optional)
- **Instructions:** Grate fresh ginger into hot water, add a pinch of turmeric, and sweeten with honey if desired. This tonic can alleviate indigestion.

Coriander and Cumin Rice:

- **Ingredients:** Basmati rice, coriander seeds, cumin seeds, ghee or olive oil, salt
- **Instructions:** Toast coriander and cumin seeds in ghee or olive oil. Add cooked basmati rice and salt. Toss to combine for a fragrant and digestive-friendly side dish.

These recipes offer a flavorful way to incorporate digestive herbs into your daily routine. Feel free to customize them to suit

your taste preferences and specific digestive
needs.

A Gentle Approach to Digestive Wellness

As you explore the world of kitchen herbs and spices for digestive health, remember that gentle, natural remedies can often be just as effective as pharmaceutical solutions. These culinary herbs offer a holistic approach to digestive harmony, nurturing your body and promoting overall well-being.

In the next chapter, we'll shift our focus to stress management and mental well-being. Discover how the aromatic herbs in your spice cabinet apothecary can help you find calm and balance in a busy world.

Chapter 6: Calm and Balance - Herbs for Stress Management

Welcome to the world of tranquility and balance, where the aromatic herbs in your spice cabinet apothecary can help you find peace in the midst of life's chaos. In this chapter, we'll explore the powerful herbs and spices that have been used for centuries to alleviate stress, anxiety, and promote mental well-being. So, whether you're dealing with the daily grind or simply seeking moments of calm, read on to discover the soothing world of herbal remedies.

Understanding Stress

Stress is an inherent part of life. It can be triggered by various factors, such as work pressures, family responsibilities, financial worries, or unexpected challenges. While some stress is normal and can even be motivating, chronic stress can take a toll on your physical and mental health.

Chronic stress may lead to:

- **Anxiety and Worry:** An ongoing sense of unease and apprehension.
- **Physical Symptoms:** Headaches, muscle tension, and digestive issues.
- **Sleep Disturbances:** Difficulty falling asleep or staying asleep.
- **Mood Swings:** Irritability, moodiness, or feelings of sadness.
- **Weakened Immune System:** Increased susceptibility to illness.

The good news is that there are natural ways to manage and reduce stress, and many of them involve the use of herbs and spices from your spice cabinet.

Herbal Allies for Stress Management

Lavender (Lavandula angustifolia):

- **Stress-Relief Benefits:** Lavender is renowned for its calming properties. It can
- **How to Use:** Create a lavender sachet for your pillow, diffuse lavender essential oil, or brew lavender tea.

Chamomile (Matricaria chamomilla):

- **Stress-Relief Benefits:** Chamomile has soothing and calming effects, making

it an excellent choice for reducing
stress and anxiety.

- **How to Use:** Make chamomile tea or
  use chamomile essential oil for
  aromatherapy.

Lemon Balm (Melissa officinalis):

- **Stress-Relief Benefits:** Lemon balm
  has mild sedative properties that can
  help relieve stress, anxiety, and
  insomnia.
- **How to Use:** Brew lemon balm tea or
  use it as a fresh herb in cooking.

Valerian (Valeriana officinalis):

- **Stress-Relief Benefits:** Valerian root is
  known for its sedative effects and can
  be helpful for managing stress-induced
  sleep problems.
- **How to Use:** Brew valerian root tea or
  take valerian supplements as directed.

Ashwagandha (Withania somnifera):

- **Stress-Relief Benefits:** Ashwagandha
  is an adaptogen that can help the body
  manage stress and reduce cortisol
  levels.
- **How to Use:** Take ashwagandha
  supplements or use it as a powdered
  herb in smoothies.

Passionflower (Passiflora incarnata):

- **Stress-Relief Benefits:** Passionflower can promote relaxation and reduce anxiety by increasing levels of gamma-aminobutyric acid (GABA) in the brain.
- **How to Use:** Brew passionflower tea or take passionflower supplements as directed.

Holy Basil (Ocimum sanctum or Ocimum tenuiflorum):

- **Stress-Relief Benefits:** Holy basil, also known as tulsi, is an adaptogen that can help the body adapt to stress and reduce anxiety.
- **How to Use:** Brew holy basil tea or take holy basil supplements as directed.

Rosemary (Rosmarinus officinalis):

- **Stress-Relief Benefits:** Rosemary has been associated with improved mood and cognitive function, making it a useful herb for stress management.
- **How to Use:** Use fresh rosemary in cooking or make rosemary-infused oil for aromatherapy.

Practical Stress-Relief Methods

Now that you're acquainted with these stress-relieving herbs, let's explore some practical methods to incorporate them into your daily routine:

Relaxing Herbal Baths:

- **Ingredients:** Lavender buds, chamomile flowers, Epsom salt
- **Instructions:** Add a handful of lavender buds, chamomile flowers, and Epsom salt to your bathwater for a soothing and aromatic soak.

Stress-Busting Herbal Teas:

- **Ingredients:** Mix and match stress-relief herbs like chamomile, lemon balm, and passionflower.
- **Instructions:** Brew a calming cup of herbal tea when you need a moment of relaxation. Sweeten with honey if desired.

Aromatherapy with Essential Oils:

- **Ingredients:** Lavender, chamomile, or rosemary essential oil
- **Instructions:** Diffuse these essential oils in your home to create a calming ambiance.

Herbal Tinctures or Supplements:

- **Ingredients:** High-quality herbal tinctures or supplements containing stress-relief herbs.
- **Instructions:** Follow the recommended dosage on the product label for stress management.

Mindful Meditation:

- **Instructions:** Practice mindfulness meditation to reduce stress and increase mental clarity. Combine it with deep breathing exercises for maximum benefit.

Herbal Potpourri:

- **Ingredients:** Dried lavender, rosemary, and lemon balm leaves
- **Instructions:** Create a fragrant potpourri mix to place in small sachets around your home or office.

Herbal Infused Oils for Massage:

- **Ingredients:** Carrier oil, lavender or chamomile flowers
- **Instructions:** Infuse carrier oil with lavender or chamomile flowers for a soothing massage oil.

Herbal Sleep Pillow:

- **Ingredients:** Dried herbs like lavender and chamomile, a small fabric pouch
- **Instructions:** Fill a small fabric pouch with dried herbs and place it under your pillow for a restful night's sleep.

Finding Your Zen

Remember that managing stress is a personal journey, and what works best for one person may differ from what works for another. Experiment with different herbs and stress-relief methods to discover your perfect blend of tranquility.

In the next chapter, we'll delve into the world of holistic wellness and explore how herbs and spices from your spice cabinet can support your overall health. Get ready to embark on a journey of well-being, one flavorful remedy at a time.

Chapter 7: Exploring Herbal Remedies for Common Ailments

Welcome to another exciting chapter in "The Spice Cabinet Apothecary: Natural Health at Your Fingertips." In this chapter, we'll delve into the practical side of herbal medicine. We'll explore how herbs and spices from your kitchen spice cabinet can be used to address common ailments and minor health issues. Get ready to discover the healing potential of nature's bounty.

Headache Relief with Peppermint:

Do you ever find yourself reaching for over-the-counter pain relievers when a headache strikes? Peppermint, a familiar spice cabinet herb, can offer a natural alternative. It contains menthol, which can help relax tense muscles in the head and neck, easing headache pain. Here's how to use it:

- **Ingredients:** Peppermint essential oil, carrier oil (such as coconut or almond oil)

- **Instructions:** Mix a few drops of peppermint essential oil with a carrier oil. Gently massage the blend onto your temples and the back of your neck. Take slow, deep breaths and let the soothing aroma work its magic.

Digestive Comfort with Ginger:

Upset stomach and digestive discomfort can be quite bothersome. Ginger, a versatile spice cabinet herb, has a long history of helping soothe these issues. Ginger contains compounds that can relax the gastrointestinal tract and reduce inflammation. Here's how to use it:

- **Ingredients:** Fresh ginger slices, hot water, honey (optional)
- **Instructions:** Grate or slice fresh ginger and steep it in hot water. Add honey for sweetness if desired. Sip this ginger tea slowly to ease digestive discomfort and nausea.

Sore Throat Relief with Honey and Cinnamon:

A sore throat can make you feel miserable. Fortunately, your spice cabinet holds two powerful allies: honey and cinnamon. Honey's natural antibacterial properties can help soothe a sore throat, while cinnamon provides a comforting flavor. Here's how to use them:

- **Ingredients:** Honey, ground cinnamon

- **Instructions:** Mix a teaspoon of honey with a pinch of ground cinnamon. Take this mixture as needed to coat and soothe your sore throat. It's not only effective but also delicious!

Cough and Cold Remedy with Thyme:

When coughs and colds strike, thyme can be a valuable ally. Thyme contains thymol, a compound with antimicrobial and antispasmodic properties. It can help calm coughs and soothe sore throats. Here's how to use it:

- **Ingredients:** Fresh or dried thyme leaves, hot water, honey (optional)
- **Instructions:** Steep fresh or dried thyme leaves in hot water to make thyme tea. Add honey for sweetness if desired. Sip this tea to ease coughs and promote recovery.

Sleep Aid with Lavender:

If you struggle with sleep, lavender can come to your rescue. Lavender's soothing aroma is known for its calming effects, making it an excellent choice for promoting better sleep. Here's how to use it:

- **Ingredients:** Dried lavender flowers, small fabric pouch

- **Instructions:** Fill a small fabric pouch with dried lavender flowers and place it under your pillow. You can also sprinkle a few drops of lavender essential oil on your pillowcase for a similar effect.

Nausea Relief with Fennel:

Nausea can be quite uncomfortable, whether it's due to motion sickness or an upset stomach. Fennel, a spice cabinet herb with a pleasant licorice-like flavor, can help ease nausea. Here's how to use it:

- **Ingredients:** Fennel seeds
- **Instructions:** Chew on a few fennel seeds or make a fennel infusion by steeping the seeds in hot water. Sip this infusion slowly to alleviate nausea.

Wound Healing with Turmeric:

Turmeric's active compound, curcumin, has potent anti-inflammatory and antibacterial properties, making it an excellent choice for wound care. Here's how to use it:
- **Ingredients:** Turmeric powder, honey
- **Instructions:** Make a paste by mixing turmeric powder with honey. Apply this paste to minor cuts, scrapes, or burns. Cover with a bandage and change it daily until the wound heals.

Anxiety and Stress Relief with Rosemary:

Feeling anxious or stressed? Rosemary, with its aromatic and calming properties, can offer relief. Here's how to use it:

- **Ingredients:** Fresh rosemary sprigs, hot water
- **Instructions:** Steep fresh rosemary sprigs in hot water to make rosemary tea. Enjoy a cup when you need to unwind and reduce anxiety.

These practical remedies are just a glimpse into the healing potential of herbs and spices found in your spice cabinet. Remember that while these remedies can be effective for minor ailments, it's important to consult a healthcare professional for more serious health concerns.

In the next chapter, we'll explore the art of crafting herbal remedies and infusions from the comfort of your kitchen. Get ready to unleash your inner herbalist and discover the joy of creating your own natural remedies.

Chapter 8: Crafting Herbal Remedies at Home From your Spice Cabinet or your Garden

Welcome to the delightful world of herbal crafting! In this chapter, we'll explore the art of creating your own herbal remedies and infusions right in the comfort of your kitchen. Whether you're a seasoned herbalist or just starting your journey, you'll discover the joy of working with nature's gifts to promote health and well-being.

The Pleasure of Crafting with Herbs

Crafting herbal remedies at home is a rewarding and empowering experience. It allows you to connect with the natural world, gain a deeper understanding of plants, and take charge of your health. Plus, there's something truly magical about transforming a handful of herbs into a healing potion or soothing infusion.

This can be done using the spices in your Spice Cabinet and/or your garden.

It is a relatively easy task to have your very own "Window sill" spice garden at your beck and call. All you need is a few containers, some good potting soil, some seeds or young plants and a window with good light. Seeds and plant starts can be found at most of the big box stores for a reasonable price as well as the potting soil and containers. If you are fortunate enough to have a front or back porch this "garden" can be expanded to meet your needs. Providing you with added benefit of the pleasure of watch your ingredients grow and mature.

Here are some reasons why you might want to try herbal crafting:

1. **Customized Remedies:** Crafting your own herbal remedies enables you to tailor them to your specific needs and preferences. You can choose the herbs that resonate with you and your well-being goals.
2. **Cost-Effective:** Making herbal remedies at home can be more cost-effective than purchasing commercial products. You can grow some herbs yourself or source them affordably.
3. **Sustainability:** By crafting your remedies, you can support sustainability by using eco-friendly practices and sourcing herbs responsibly.
4. **Empowerment:** Herbal crafting empowers you to take an active role in your health and

wellness. You become your own herbalist, making decisions about what goes into your remedies.

Essential Tools for Herbal Crafting

Before we dive into crafting specific remedies, let's ensure you have the essential tools and ingredients for your herbal journey. Here's what you'll need:

1. **Dried Herbs:** Start with a selection of dried herbs like lavender, chamomile, rosemary, peppermint, and thyme. You can purchase these or dry your own fresh herbs.
2. Fresh Herbs: If you have access to fresh herbs from your garden or local market, they can add vibrancy to your creations.
3. **Carrier Oils:** Carrier oils like coconut oil, olive oil, and almond oil are essential for making herbal-infused oils, salves, and balms.
4. **Essential Oils:** These concentrated plant extracts add fragrance and therapeutic properties to your remedies. Common essential oils include lavender, tea tree, eucalyptus, and lemon.
5. **Dried Flowers and Leaves:** These can be used for making herbal teas, bath blends, or potpourri. Examples include dried rose petals, calendula flowers, and lemon balm leaves.

6. **Glass Jars and Bottles:** Glass containers are ideal for storing your herbal creations as they don't interact with the herbs and essential oils.
7. **Strainers and Cheesecloth:** These are necessary for filtering herbal infusions and oils.

Labels: Don't forget to label your creations with the herb used, date of preparation, and usage instructions.

<u>Basic Herbal Crafting Techniques</u>

Now, let's explore some basic herbal crafting techniques that you can use to create a variety of remedies:

Herbal Infusions:

Herbal infusions are concentrated herbal teas that can be used for various purposes, such as soothing a sore throat or promoting relaxation.

- **Ingredients:** Dried herbs or flowers, hot water
- **Instructions:** Place the herbs in a glass jar and cover with hot water. Allow them to steep for a specific duration, usually 15-30 minutes. Strain and use the infused liquid.

-

Herbal Tinctures:

Tinctures are alcohol-based extracts that preserve the medicinal properties of herbs. They are convenient and have a longer shelf life.

- **Ingredients:** Dried herbs, alcohol (such as vodka or brandy)
- **Instructions:** Fill a glass jar with dried herbs and cover with alcohol. Seal the jar and let it sit for 2-6 weeks, shaking it occasionally. Strain and store the liquid in a dark glass dropper bottle.

Herbal Salves:

Salves are semi-solid ointments that can be applied topically. They're great for skin issues, such as minor cuts, scrapes, and dry skin.

- **Ingredients:** Herbal-infused oil, beeswax
- **Instructions:** Heat the infused oil and beeswax in a double boiler until the wax melts. Pour the mixture into containers and let it cool and solidify.
-

Herbal Bath Blends:

Herbal baths are a luxurious way to relax and nourish your skin. They can also help alleviate muscle soreness and stress.

- **Ingredients:** Dried herbs, Epsom salt, baking soda (optional)
- **Instructions:** Mix dried herbs with Epsom salt and baking soda (optional). Place the blend in a muslin bag or tie it in a cloth for an herbal bath sachet.

Herbal Potpourri:

Herbal potpourri adds a delightful fragrance to your living space. It's simple to make and can be customized with your favorite herbs and flowers.

- **Ingredients:** Dried herbs, dried flowers, essential oils (optional)
- **Instructions:** Combine dried herbs and flowers in a bowl. Add a few drops of essential oil if desired. Place the mixture in a decorative dish or sachet.

Crafting Your First Herbal Remedy

Now that you have the tools and techniques, let's create your first herbal remedy: a soothing lavender-infused oil.

Lavender-Infused Oil:

Lavender-infused oil is a versatile remedy that can be used for massage, relaxation, or as a base for homemade salves and balms.

Ingredients:

- Dried lavender flowers
- Carrier oil (e.g., almond oil, olive oil)
- Glass jar with a lid

Instructions:

1. Fill a glass jar halfway with dried lavender flowers.
2. Pour the carrier oil over the lavender flowers, ensuring they are completely submerged.
3. Seal the jar with a tight-fitting lid.
4. Place the jar in a warm, sunny spot for 2-4 weeks, shaking it gently every day.
5. After the infusion period, strain the oil through cheesecloth or a fine mesh strainer to remove the lavender flowers.
6. Transfer the lavender-infused oil to a clean glass container with a lid.
7. Label the container with the contents and date of preparation.

Your lavender-infused oil is now ready to use. You can apply it to your skin for a calming massage, add a few drops to your bath, or use it as a base for creating other lavender-infused products.

Exploring Endless Possibilities

Herbal crafting is an exploration of endless possibilities. As you become more confident in your skills, you can create an array of herbal remedies, from herbal salves and lip balms to herbal teas and fragrant sachets. Remember that crafting with herbs is not only about the end product but also about the journey of discovery and connection with nature.

1. Chamomile and Lavender Sleepy Time Tea:

This delightful herbal tea blend is perfect for winding down after a long day, promoting relaxation, and improving sleep quality.

Ingredients:

- 1 tablespoon dried chamomile flowers
- 1 tablespoon dried lavender buds
- 1 cup hot water
- Honey (optional, for sweetness)

Instructions:

1. Place the dried chamomile and lavender in a tea infuser or a teapot.
2. Pour hot water over the herbs and steep for about 5-7 minutes.

3. Remove the infuser or strain the tea to remove the herbs.
4. If desired, add honey for sweetness.
5. Sip and enjoy this calming tea before bedtime.

2. Peppermint and Ginger Digestive Tea:

This herbal tea blend combines the digestive powers of peppermint and ginger to soothe an upset stomach and aid digestion.

Ingredients:

- 1 tablespoon dried peppermint leaves
- 1 teaspoon dried ginger root (or a few thin slices of fresh ginger)
- 1 cup hot water
- Lemon or honey (optional, for flavor)

Instructions:

1. Place the dried peppermint and ginger in a tea infuser or a teapot.
2. Pour hot water over the herbs and steep for about 5-10 minutes.
3. Remove the infuser or strain the tea to remove the herbs.
4. Optionally, add a squeeze of lemon or a drizzle of honey for extra flavor.
5. Sip this soothing tea to ease digestive discomfort.

3. Rosemary and Eucalyptus Steam Inhalation:

This steam inhalation blend can help relieve congestion, clear the sinuses, and ease respiratory discomfort.

Ingredients:

- 2 tablespoons dried rosemary leaves
- 2-3 drops eucalyptus essential oil
- Boiling water

Instructions:

1. Place the dried rosemary in a heatproof bowl.
2. Add the eucalyptus essential oil to the bowl.
3. Carefully pour boiling water over the herbs and oil.
4. Lean over the bowl, covering your head with a towel to create a tent, and inhale the steam for 5-10 minutes.
5. This inhalation can help clear your airways and provide relief from congestion.

4. Lavender and Oatmeal Bath Soak:

This soothing bath blend combines the relaxation benefits of lavender with the skin-nourishing qualities of oatmeal.

Ingredients:

* 1/2 cup dried lavender flowers
* 1 cup rolled oats.
* Muslin bag or cheesecloth

Instructions:

1. Combine the dried lavender flowers and rolled oats in a muslin bag or cheesecloth.
2. Tie the bag securely to create a sachet.
3. Hang the sachet under the faucet as you fill your bath with warm water.
4. Let the water flow through the sachet, releasing the lavender and oatmeal into the bath.
5. Enjoy a relaxing soak in this fragrant and skin-soothing bath.

5. Calendula Healing Salve:

This herbal salve is excellent for promoting the healing of minor cuts, scrapes, and dry skin.

Ingredients:

* 1/4 cup dried calendula petals
* 1/2 cup carrier oil (such as olive oil or coconut oil)
* 1-2 tablespoons beeswax pellets

Instructions:

1. Combine the dried calendula petals and carrier oil in a glass jar.
2. Seal the jar and place it in a sunny spot for about 2 weeks, shaking it gently daily.
3. After infusing, strain the oil to remove the calendula petals.
4. In a double boiler, gently heat the calendula-infused oil and add beeswax pellets. Stir until the beeswax melts and the mixture thickens slightly.
5. Pour the salve into clean containers and allow it to cool and solidify.
6. Use this soothing calendula salve for minor skin irritations and dry patches.

These herbal recipes offer a taste of the creative and healing potential of crafting with herbs at home. Enjoy the process of making and using these remedies to enhance your well-being naturally.

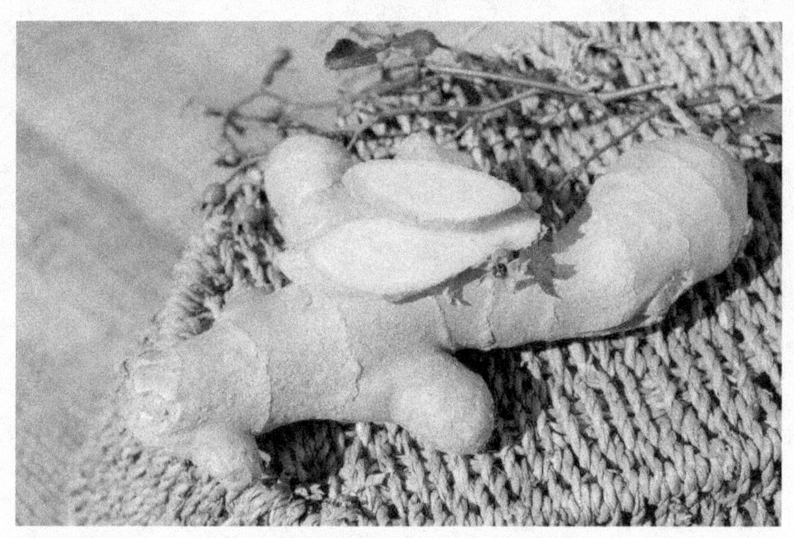

Chapter 9: The Art of Herbal Tea Blending

Welcome to the wonderful world of herbal tea blending, where creativity meets wellness! In this chapter, we'll explore the art of crafting your own herbal tea blends. Herbal teas are not only delicious and comforting; they can also offer a wide range of health benefits. Get ready to unleash your inner herbalist and discover the joy of creating unique and flavorful herbal tea combinations.

The Magic of Herbal Tea Blending

Herbal teas, also known as tisanes, have been enjoyed for centuries for their soothing properties and natural flavors. What makes herbal tea blending so magical is the ability to mix and match different herbs, spices, flowers, and fruits to create a blend that suits your taste preferences and wellness goals.

Why blend your own herbal teas?

1. **Personalized Flavors:** You can tailor your tea blends to your taste, experimenting with various combinations until you find the perfect flavor profile.

2. **Health Benefits:** Different herbs and botanicals offer unique health benefits, allowing you to craft teas that support your well-being.
3. **Creativity:** Herbal tea blending is a form of culinary art. It's an opportunity to express your creativity and connect with nature.

Essential Tools for Herbal Tea Blending

Before we dive into the art of blending, let's make sure you have the essential tools for crafting your herbal teas:

1. **Dried Herbs:** Collect a variety of dried herbs, flowers, and spices to use as your base ingredients.
2. **Fresh Herbs and Fruits:** Fresh ingredients can add vibrancy and depth to your blends. Consider mint leaves, citrus zest, or fresh berries.
3. **Tea Infusers or Strainers:** These are essential for steeping loose herbs and preventing bits from floating in your tea.
4. **Airtight Containers:** Store your blended teas in airtight containers to preserve their freshness and flavor.
5. **Labels:** Don't forget to label your blends with their ingredients and brewing instructions.

Creating Your Herbal Tea Blends

Now, let's dive into the art of crafting herbal tea blends. We'll start with some classic blends and then explore how to experiment and create your own signature teas.

Classic Herbal Tea Blends:

Chamomile and Lavender Relaxation Blend:

- **Ingredients:** Dried chamomile flowers, dried lavender buds
- **Instructions:** Mix equal parts of dried chamomile and lavender. Steep a teaspoon of the blend in hot water for 5-7 minutes. This soothing tea is perfect for winding down.

Peppermint and Lemon Balm Digestive Aid:

- **Ingredients:** Dried peppermint leaves, dried lemon balm leaves
- **Instructions:** Combine equal parts of dried peppermint and lemon balm. Steep a teaspoon of the blend in hot water for 5-10 minutes. Sip after meals for digestion support.

Ginger and Turmeric Immune Booster:

- **Ingredients:** Dried ginger root, dried turmeric root, black pepper (for absorption)
- **Instructions:** Mix ginger and turmeric in a 2:1 ratio and add a pinch of black pepper. Steep a teaspoon of the blend in hot water for 10-15 minutes. This warming tea can boost your immune system.

Creating Your Signature Blends:

1. **Taste Testing:** Begin by tasting your individual herbs and spices to understand their flavor profiles. Note which ones are earthy, floral, minty, or spicy.
2. **Balance:** Think about the balance of flavors you want to achieve. A well-balanced tea blend might combine sweet and spicy or floral and citrusy notes.
3. **Health Goals:** Consider your wellness goals. Do you want to create a calming bedtime blend or an invigorating morning tea to kickstart your day?
4. **Experiment:** Start with a base ingredient (like chamomile or green tea) and add complementary herbs and spices. Experiment with ratios until you achieve the desired taste and aroma.
5. **Keep Records:** As you create blends, keep notes on the ingredients and ratios you use. This will help you replicate successful blends in the future.

Herbal Tea Blending Inspiration:

Here are a few inspirational ideas to get you started:

- **Floral Fantasy:** Combine rose petals, hibiscus, and lavender for a fragrant and visually stunning tea blend.
- **Citrus Burst:** Mix dried orange peel, lemon verbena, and a touch of mint for a zesty and uplifting tea.
- **Spice Delight:** Create a warming blend with cinnamon, cardamom, and cloves. Add a hint of black tea or rooibos for depth.
- **Garden Medley:** Use fresh herbs like basil, thyme, and sage along with dried chamomile for a unique garden-inspired tea.
- **Berry Bliss:** Blend dried hibiscus flowers, dried berries, and a touch of rosehip for a fruity and vitamin-rich tea.

Brewing Your Herbal Blends:

Once you've crafted your herbal tea blends, here's how to brew the perfect cup:

1. **Measure:** Use about 1-2 teaspoons of your herbal blend for every 8 ounces of hot water.

2. **Boil Water:** Heat water to the appropriate temperature for your blend. Different herbs require different water temperatures, so consult your ingredient's guidelines.
3. **Steep:** Place your blend in a tea infuser or strainer and pour the hot water over it.
4. **Cover and Wait:** Cover your cup or teapot and let the tea steep for the recommended time (usually 5-10 minutes).
5. **Sip and Savor:** Remove the infuser or strain the tea, and enjoy your aromatic and flavorful creation.

Safety Note: While herbal teas are generally safe, some herbs may interact with medications or have contraindications for certain medical conditions. If you have health concerns or are pregnant or nursing, it's advisable to consult a healthcare professional before regularly consuming herbal teas.

As you embark on your journey of herbal tea blending, remember that there are no strict rules—just your creativity and personal preferences. Whether you're crafting teas for relaxation, digestion, or pure enjoyment, the art of herbal tea blending offers a delightful way to connect with nature and enhance your well-being, one sip at a time.

Chapter 10: Herbs for Every Season

Welcome to the final chapter of your herbal journey, where we'll explore the magic of herbs for every season. Throughout this book, you've learned about the remarkable properties of herbs and spices and how to incorporate them into your daily life. Now, let's dive deeper into the seasonal aspects of herbalism, discovering how nature's bounty changes with the rhythm of the year and how you can harness these changes for your well-being.

The Seasonal Dance of Nature

Each season brings its unique energy, climate, and opportunities for growth and transformation. Herbs and spices are deeply attuned to these changes, adapting their properties and flavors accordingly. Understanding this seasonal dance can deepen your connection with nature and enhance the effectiveness of your herbal remedies.

<u>Spring: Renewal and Cleansing</u>

Spring is a time of rebirth, as the earth awakens from its winter slumber. It's a season of renewal, growth, and cleansing. The herbs of spring often have a detoxifying and invigorating quality, perfect for shedding the heaviness of winter.

Herbs of Spring:

1. **Dandelion:** Known for its detoxifying properties, dandelion leaves and roots can be used in teas and salads to support liver health and digestion.
2. **Nettle:** Rich in vitamins and minerals, nettle is a nourishing herb that can be consumed in soups, teas, or as a sautéed green.
3. **Cleavers:** This herb is a gentle lymphatic cleanser and can be used in teas to support the body's natural detoxification processes.
4. **Mint:** Mint's fresh and invigorating flavor makes it an excellent choice for teas and beverages to awaken the senses.

Summer: Vibrancy and Vitality

Summer is a time of vibrancy, with longer days and bountiful sunshine. Herbs of summer often have cooling and refreshing properties, making them perfect for staying hydrated and maintaining vitality.

Herbs of Summer:

1. **Lemon Balm:** Known for its soothing qualities, lemon balm makes a delightful tea that calms the nerves and uplifts the spirit.
2. **Lavender:** Lavender's aromatic blooms can be used to make soothing teas and aromatherapy blends for relaxation.
3. **Rose:** The petals of the rose can be infused into water for a refreshing and uplifting summer drink.
4. **Basil:** Fresh basil is a staple in summer cuisine, adding flavor and aroma to salads, sauces, and drinks.

Autumn: Harvest and Grounding

Autumn heralds the harvest season, where herbs are at their peak of potency. It's a time of grounding, as we prepare for the cooler months ahead. Herbs of autumn often have warming and nourishing properties.

Herbs of Autumn:

1. **Echinacea:** Often used to support the immune system, echinacea can be made into teas or tinctures to help ward off seasonal illnesses.

2. **Ginger:** With its warming quality, ginger is a favorite for soothing teas and adding spice to autumn dishes.
3. **Cinnamon:** The comforting aroma of cinnamon is perfect for spiced teas, baked goods, and warming beverages.
4. **Elderberry:** Elderberry syrup or tea is a popular remedy for boosting the immune system during the colder months.

Winter: Comfort and Resilience

Winter is a time of hibernation and introspection. Herbs of winter often have comforting and fortifying qualities, helping us stay resilient during the chilliest months.

Herbs of Winter:

1. **Chamomile:** Chamomile's calming properties make it an ideal choice for soothing bedtime teas that promote restful sleep.
2. **Peppermint:** Peppermint's invigorating flavor can uplift the spirits and support digestion, especially after hearty holiday meals.
3. **Thyme:** Thyme is a traditional remedy for respiratory issues, often used in soothing cough syrups and teas.
4. **Cayenne:** A pinch of cayenne can add warmth and spice to winter dishes and help improve circulation.

Year-Round Herbs: The Herbal Allies

While herbs have their unique seasonal specialties, some herbs are versatile and can be enjoyed throughout the year. These herbal allies can provide consistent support to your well-being, regardless of the season.

Year-Round Herbs:

1. **Rosemary:** Rosemary's robust flavor enhances a variety of dishes and can be used in teas, infusions, and topical remedies.
2. **Lemon:** Fresh lemon juice and zest can add a burst of citrusy flavor to your beverages and culinary creations.
3. **Garlic:** Garlic is not only a culinary staple but also a powerful medicinal herb with immune-boosting properties.
4. **Turmeric:** Known for its anti-inflammatory benefits, turmeric can be used in cooking, teas, and wellness elixirs year-round.
5.

Seasonal Herbal Rituals

As you deepen your connection with herbs through the seasons, consider incorporating seasonal herbal rituals into your life:

- **Spring Cleansing:** In spring, embrace cleansing herbal teas and incorporate rituals like spring cleaning and decluttering to align with the season of renewal.
- **Summer Self-Care:** Use summer herbs to create refreshing skincare products and enjoy outdoor rituals that celebrate the sun's energy.
- **Autumn Harvest:** Harvest and preserve herbs for winter use, and practice gratitude rituals to honor the season of abundance.
- **Winter Comfort:** Embrace cozy herbal teas and self-care practices like meditation and journaling to nurture your inner world.

By embracing the wisdom of herbs in every season, you can enhance your well-being, deepen your connection with nature, and create a more harmonious and balanced life.

Conclusion: Your Herbal Journey

Congratulations on completing your herbal journey through ***"The Spice Cabinet Apothecary: Natural Health at Your Fingertips."*** You've learned how herbs and spices from your kitchen spice cabinet can be potent allies in your quest for health and wellness. Whether you're sipping a soothing herbal tea, crafting your own remedies, or embracing the seasons through herbs, you've discovered the profound ways in which nature's gifts can enhance your life.

As you continue your herbal exploration, remember that your journey is ongoing. Nature has an infinite treasury of herbs and spices waiting for you to discover. Keep experimenting, learning, and connecting with the remarkable world of herbalism. Your path to natural health is a beautiful and lifelong adventure.

Thank you for joining us on this journey, and may your life be filled with the vibrant health and well-being that herbs and spices offer.

Other Books By Richard D. Krause

"The Elderly Trap: Uncovering Scams and Reclaiming Security in the Golden Years"

"The Art of Personal Mastery: A Roadmap to Success and Fulfillment"

"From Words to Wealth, Mastering Freelance Writing"

"The Writers Odyssey: Crafting Your Literary Legacy, A New Writer's Guide Book"

"The Morning Elixir of Life: The History and Art of Coffee"

"EBook Entrepreneur: Crafting Your Path to Profit"

Please Visit Mr. Krause's website at rkrause45.wixsite.com/mysite for a complete updated list of his works.